MW00680777

Little Giant—Children's Bible Classics
Copyright © 1992 by Educational Publishing Concepts, Inc.

(ISBN 0-529-07195-9)
Printed in Singapore

CONTENTS

JESUS' LAST WEEK

THE CHURCH BEGINS

PAUL'S MISSIONARY JOURNEYS

Jesus Cleans the Temple *Mark 11:1-19*

Jesus and His disciples were traveling to Jerusalem.
When they got to the Mount of Olives, which is right
outside the city, they stopped.

5

Jesus sent two disciples into a nearby village saying, "There is a young colt tied up there. Bring it to Me. If anyone questions why you are taking it just say that the Lord needs it and will return it later."

6

The disciples went into the city and found the colt, just as Jesus said they would. As they were untying it someone did ask them, "What are you doing untying that colt?"

They gave the answer Jesus had told them and they
were permitted to take the colt. They brought the colt to
Jesus and threw their coats and robes over it's back.
Jesus got on and rode toward Jerusalem.

8

As they headed toward the city, many people spread their coats out on the road in front of Jesus. Others cut large palm branches from the fields and spread them before Him.

The crowds surrounded Jesus and all the people were
shouting, "Hosanna! Blessed is He who comes in the
name of the Lord! Blessed is the return of our father
David's kingdom! Hosanna!"

This is the way that Jesus entered the city of Jerusa-lem. When He had sent the colt home, He went to the temple and looked around. Then because it was almost evening, He went out to Bethany for the night.

The next day Jesus returned to the temple in Jerusalem. This time He went to all the people who were buying and selling things there. He began to drive them out of the temple.

12

He turned over the tables of the moneychangers and the chairs of the ones selling birds. He wouldn't let anyone carry anything out of the temple.

Jesus said, "Is it not written, 'My house shall be a house of prayer for all nations'? But you have turned it into a den of robbers."

14

When the chief priests and scribes heard about this,
they started talking again about a way to kill Jesus.
The problem was many of the people liked Him, and
trying to hurt Him might start a riot.

So they didn't do anything to Jesus that day. When evening came Jesus and His disciples left the city.

The Last Supper *John 13:2-15; Mark 14:17-25*

One night while the disciples were busy preparing the
Passover supper, Jesus took off His outer coat and
tucked a towel around His waist.

Then He filled a big bowl with water and began to wash the feet of the disciples. He used the towel around His waist to dry their feet.

18

When it was Peter's turn he said, "Lord, You shouldn't be washing our feet like this!" Jesus answered, "Unless I wash you, you have no part with Me."

"In that case wash my head and my hands, too, not just my feet," Peter cried. "A person who has had a bath needs only his feet washed to be clean," Jesus replied.

20

When He had washed all the disciples' feet, Jesus put His robe back on and once again took His place at the table. "Do you understand what I have done for you?" He asked.

"You call Me Teacher and Lord. Now that I, your
Teacher and Lord, have washed your feet, you also
should wash one another's feet. I have set an example
for you."

"This is the truth, no servant is greater than his master, and no messenger is greater than the one who sent him. Now that you know these things; do them and you will be blessed."

Later as they were eating the meal Jesus said, "One of you here is going to betray Me." The disciples looked around wondering which one of them He meant. Then He said, "It is the one I give this bread to."

Jesus gave the bread to Judas Iscariot. Judas took the bread then got up and hurried out of the room. The other disciples didn't understand what was going on, but Jesus knew.

As they were eating together, Jesus took a loaf of bread in His hands. He blessed it and broke it into pieces. He gave each disciple a piece and said, "Take this and eat it, it is My body."

Then He took a cup and gave thanks for it. He passed it to each of the disciples, who all drank from it. Jesus said, "This is My blood which seals the new promise between God and man; it is poured out for many."

"Truly I will not drink the fruit of the vine again until I drink a new kind in the kingdom of God."

Jesus is Betrayed *Mark 14:26-50; John 18:10-11*

28

Jesus and His disciples ate the Passover meal together in the upper room. When they finished eating, they sang a hymn together. After that all of them except Judas Iscariot went to the Mount of Olives.

When they got there Jesus said to the disciples, "You will all desert Me. But after I am raised up, I will go before you to Galilee."

Peter quickly declared, "Even if everyone else leaves You, I will not!"

Jesus replied, "Today, before the rooster crows twice, you will deny Me three times."

32

But Peter shouted, "Even if I have to die for You, I will not deny You!" All the other disciples said the same thing.

Jesus took the disciples to a place called Gethsemane.
He told them to wait there while He went to pray. He
took Peter, James and John with Him.

34

Jesus began to pray and He became very upset and troubled. He turned to His three disciples and said, "I am overwhelmed with sorrow. Stay here and keep watch."

He went on a little way from the three and knelt on the ground. He prayed, "Father, I know that everything is possible for You. Take this cup from Me, yet I want Your will to be done, not Mine."

36

When Jesus had finished praying, He returned to the
three disciples. He found them sleeping. He woke Peter
and asked, "Couldn't you stay awake for just an hour?
Watch and pray so that you do not fall into temptation."

Jesus went away and prayed a second time. Again when He returned the disciples were sleeping. This even happened a third time. Finally He said, "Get up! The time has come, My betrayer is here."

38

Judas was approaching with a group of soldiers who had been sent by the Jewish religious leaders. He went right up to Jesus and kissed Him on the cheek.

The kiss was the signal, and the soldiers grabbed
Jesus. Peter drew his sword and cut off the ear of
Malchus, the high priest's servant. Then everyone ran
away, leaving Jesus alone with His enemies.

Peter Denies Jesus *Mark 14:53-72*

Jesus was arrested in the garden of Gethsemane and taken to the home of the high priest. All the chief priests and Jewish leaders were there waiting for Him. This was the Sanhedrin or the Jewish court.

Peter was following the group from a distance. When they reached the house, where the trial would be. He went into the courtyard of the house. He warmed himself by the fire.

Jesus' enemies had searched to find witnesses who would testify against Him so that they could put Him to death. But they couldn't find even two witnesses whose testimonies agreed.

Finally two men stood up and told this lie about Jesus.
"We heard Him say that He would destroy the temple
that is made with hands, and in three days He would
build a new one, not made with hands."

44

The high priest turned to Jesus and asked, "What about the things these men have said about You? Don't You have an answer?" But Jesus did not say a word.

The high priest asked, "Are You the Christ, the Son of God?" "I am," Jesus answered, "And you will see the Son of man sitting at God's right hand and coming with the clouds of heaven."

46

The high priest tore his garment and cried, "Why do you need anymore witnesses? You have heard His blasphemy. What is your decision?"

They all decided that Jesus deserved to die. Then
some began to spit on Him, they blindfolded Him and
hit Him saying, "Go on Prophet, tell us who hit You
that time?"

48

About the same time one of the servants of the high priest saw Peter out in the courtyard. She said, "I know you, you were with that Nazarene, Jesus." Peter denied it, "I don't know what you are talking about."

She turned to the others standing around and said, "This man was with the Nazarene, he is one of them." Again, Peter denied it.

50

A little while later some men said, "You must be one of
them because you are a Galilean." Peter denied it, "I am
telling you that I don't know what you are talking
about!"

Just then Peter heard the rooster crow twice and he remembered what Jesus had said, "You will deny Me three times before the rooster crows twice." Peter fell down and cried.

Jesus Is Condemned *John 18:28—19:16*

52

The Jewish leaders had questioned Jesus all night.
Now, very early in the morning, they brought Him to
the palace of Pilate, the Roman governor. They didn't go
in because of fear that they would be defiled.

So Pilate came out to them and asked, "What are your charges against this Man?" The priests said, "If He were not a criminal we wouldn't have brought Him to you. But we want Him executed and we need your approval."

54

Pilate went back inside and spoke to Jesus, "Are You the king of the Jews?" he asked. Jesus said, "My kingdom is not on earth, if it were My servants would have fought My arrest. It is from another place."

"You are a king then," Pilate said. "Yes I am a king," Jesus said. "I was born to bring truth to the world." "What is truth?" Pilate asked.

56

Pilate went out to the people and said, "I find no reason to charge this Man with anything. But as is my custom, I will release one prisoner at the Passover. Shall I release this 'king of the Jews?' "

The crowd began shouting, "No, not Him. We want Barabbas free!" (Barabbas was a Jew who had been arrested for murder.)

So Pilate had Jesus beaten. The soldiers made a crown
from thorns and put on His head, and they put a
scarlet robe on His back. They scornfully cried, "Hail,
King of the Jews," and they slapped His face.

Pilate went to the people once more and said, "Look, I find no wrong in this Man." He brought Jesus out, wearing the crown of thorns and the scarlet robe. When the people saw Him they cried, "Crucify Him, crucify Him!"

60

But Pilate said, "If you want Him crucified, you take Him and do it. I find no basis for any charge against Him." The priests insisted, "According to our law He must die because He claimed to be the Son of God."

When Pilate heard this, he became frightened. He tried to set Jesus free, but the priests shouted, "If you free Him, you are not Caesar's friend. Anyone who claims to be a king is Caesar's enemy."

62

So Pilate sat down on his judgment seat and Jesus was brought before him. "Here is your king," he said to the Jews. "Take Him away. Crucify Him," they cried.

"You want me to crucify your king?" Pilate asked. "We have no king but Caesar," the people responded. So finally Pilate gave Jesus over to be crucified.

Jesus is Crucified Mark 15:16-41

Pilate had agreed to crucify Jesus so he handed Him over to the soldiers. They took Jesus back into the palace and made fun of Him saying, "Hail, King of the Jews." They hit Him on the head and some spit on Him.

Finally, they took the scarlet robe off Him and put His own clothes back on Him. Then they took Him out to where He would be crucified.

66

A man from Cyrene named Simon happened to be passing by at that time. The soldiers grabbed him and made him carry Jesus' cross.

They came to the place called the Skull or Golgotha.
Then they nailed Jesus' hands and feet to the cross and
lifted it up and dropped it into the ground. This was at
about nine o'clock in the morning.

The soldiers divided up His clothes, even gambling to
see who would get His robe.

A sign was put above Jesus' head stating the reason He was being crucified. It read, "The King of the Jews." Two robbers were being crucified at the same time. One was on His right and one was on His left.

People who passed by made fun of Jesus. "You were going to destroy the temple and rebuild it in three days," they said, "Let's see You save Yourself first!"

The religious leaders mocked Him, too. "He was so great at saving others, but He can't save Himself. Come on down, King of Israel, so we can believe."

Suddenly at about twelve o'clock darkness fell over the whole land. It lasted for three hours.

Then at about three o'clock, Jesus cried out, "My God, My God, why have You forsaken Me?" Shortly after that He gave a loud cry and died.

74

Standing a little way off some of Jesus' friends were watching. Among them were Mary Magdalene, Mary the mother of James and Joseph, Salome, and other women who had come from Galilee to Jerusalem with Jesus.

When the Roman centurion who was standing in front
of Jesus saw how He died, he said, "This Man surely
was the Son of God."

Jesus is Alive! *Matthew 27:57—28:10*

Jesus had died, nailed to a cross between two robbers.

That night a follower of Jesus named Joseph of
Arimathea went to Pilate, the Roman governor. He
wanted to take the body of Jesus and prepare it for
burial. Pilate gave his permission.

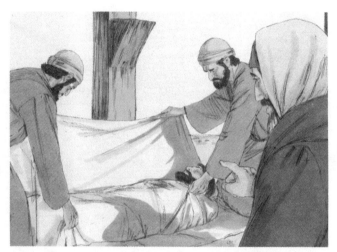

So Joseph took the body of Jesus down from the cross.
He wrapped it in a clean linen cloth and placed it in his
own tomb. This tomb was cut out of rock and had
never been used.

The chief priests and Pharisees, who had hated Jesus, went to see Pilate one more time. They said, "We remember that this liar once said that after three days He would come back to life again."

"We are afraid that His disciples will go in and steal His
body and try to make it look like He has risen from the
dead." So Pilate gave them guards to place beside the
tomb and they closed the door of the tomb so it couldn't
be opened.

On Sunday morning, the third day after Jesus' death, Mary Magdalene and some others came to the tomb where Jesus was buried. They had been there when the huge stone was rolled in place to seal the entrance of the tomb.

As the women approached, there was a great earthquake and an angel of the Lord came and rolled back
the stone and sat on it. The guards shook with fear and
fell down like dead men.

The angel spoke to the women, "Don't be afraid. I know that you are looking for Jesus who was crucified. He is not here, He is risen as He said."

84

"Come in and see where His body was laying," the angel said.

Then the angel told them to quickly go and tell His disciples that He is alive and He is going ahead of them to Galilee. "You will see Him there," the angel said.

86

The women quickly ran away from the tomb to tell His disciples. They were filled with wonderful joy, yet they were afraid too.

Suddenly Jesus was standing in front of them. They fell to the ground and worshiped Him. "Don't be afraid," Jesus said. "Tell My brothers to go to Galilee and I will meet them there."

Two Men See Jesus *Luke 24:13-35*

The risen Jesus had appeared to Mary Magdalene and the other women at the tomb. They had run to tell the disciples that Jesus was risen, but the disciples had trouble believing the news.

That same day two of Jesus' disciples were walking on the road to Emmaus, a small village about seven miles from Jerusalem. They were quietly talking about all the things that had happened.

90

As they were talking, Jesus Himself came up and began walking with them. But they did not even recognize Him because God kept them from doing so.

Jesus asked, "What are you two talking about as you walk along?" The two men stopped walking, their faces filled with sadness. "Don't you know everything that has happened in Jerusalem the last few days?" they asked.

"Our own chief priests and rulers handed over Jesus of Nazareth to be crucified. He was a mighty prophet and did wonderful miracles before God and all people."

"We all believed that He was the Messiah, the one to save Israel. What's more, this morning some women from our group went to His tomb. But, He was gone, His body is missing."

94

"The women even say that they saw an angel who told them that Jesus is alive, that He rose from the dead. Some of our men went to see and indeed, the tomb was empty, but they did not see Him."

Jesus said, "You foolish men, why can't you believe all that the prophets wrote so long ago? Didn't they predict that the Messiah would have to suffer all these things and enter into His glory?"

Then Jesus began to explain the Scriptures to them.
He began with Moses and the prophets and explained
everything that had to do with Him.

When they arrived in Emmaus, it seemed like Jesus
was going on further. The two men asked Him to stay
with them because it was almost evening. So Jesus
stayed with them.

98

They prepared some food and as they were eating,
Jesus took some bread, blessed it and broke it. As He
gave it to them, God suddenly let them recognize Him.
They got up at once and returned to Jerusalem.

When they joined the other disciples, they were told that Jesus had appeared to Peter. They shared their story of Jesus' appearance to them. It was true! Jesus was really alive!

Christ Appears Luke 24:36-53

Jesus had risen from the dead. He had appeared to some of His disciples at different times. But one of them, Thomas, had never been with the others when they saw Jesus.

They had told Thomas about seeing Jesus. But, Thomas said, "I won't believe He is alive until I see the nailprints in His hands and touch His side myself."

102

About a week later, all the disciples, including Thomas, were in a locked room together. Suddenly, they realized Jesus was standing there with them. He said, "Peace be with you."

Jesus knew what Thomas had said before, so He said, "Here Thomas, see My hands, touch My side. Stop doubting Thomas, and believe." Now Thomas did believe and he said, "My Lord and my God!"

104

Jesus said, "Thomas, you believe because you have seen Me. Those who have not seen Me and still believe are very blessed!"

One other time Jesus appeared to the disciples on a mountaintop in Galilee. He told them, "I have been given all authority in heaven and on earth. So, go tell everyone and make disciples in all the nations."

"Baptize all believers in the name of the Father, Son and the Holy Spirit. Teach them all that I have taught you. Remember that I will be with you always."

Jesus appeared again to the disciples in Jerusalem. This time He asked them for something to eat. They gave Him some fish and He ate it in front of them.

108

Jesus reminded them that He had told them before His crucifixion that everything written about Him in the law of Moses and by the prophets would come true.

"They have written that the Christ would suffer and die and on the third day He would rise from the dead. Repentance and forgiveness in His name would be preached to all nations."

110

"You are My witnesses of these things and you shall receive power from God My Father."

Jesus took them to Bethany. He blessed them and then left them. The disciples went back to Jerusalem full of happiness and praising God.

Jesus Goes to Heaven *Acts 1*

For forty days after His resurrection, Jesus appeared to His disciples at different times. He encouraged them and told them about the kingdom of God.

On one occasion He told them, "Stay in Jerusalem and wait for the gift the Father has promised you. In a few days you will be baptized with the Holy Spirit."

114

The disciples asked Him, "Lord are You going to restore the kingdom to Israel now?" Jesus answered, "The Father has made those arrangements and it is not for you to know the times or dates He has set."

"But you will receive power when the Holy Spirit comes on you," He continued. "And you will tell people about me in Jerusalem, and in Judea and Samaria and on every part of the earth."

116

As Jesus was saying this He was taken up away from them until a cloud completely covered Him. The disciples were still studying the sky when two angels appeared beside them.

The angels said, "What are you staring at? This same Jesus who has gone up to heaven will come back in the same way."

So the disciples returned to Jerusalem. They all stayed together, except Judas. Also with them was Mary, Jesus' mother, some other women and some of His brothers. They spent much of their time in prayer.

Judas was now dead. After betraying Jesus for a mere thirty pieces of silver, he bought a field with the money. He hanged himself there in that very field.

120

"It is necessary to replace Judas," Peter announced. "We must choose someone who has been with us from the time of Jesus' baptism until the time when He was taken up from us to be a witness of the resurrection."

Two men were suggested. One was Barsabbas, also known as Justus. The other was Matthias.

They all prayed together, "Lord, show us Your will. You know what is in every heart. Which of these two have You chosen to take over the work of an apostle?"

So they drew lots and the choice was Matthias and he was added to the group of apostles in place of Judas.

The Holy Spirit Comes *Acts 2*

The Day of Pentecost had come and all of Jesus' followers were gathered together in Jerusalem. It had only been ten days since He had been taken up into heaven.

Suddenly they all heard a sound that was like a strong wind blowing, and they saw flames of fire that moved around and settled on each of them. They all began to speak in different languages.

126

Many godly Jews were in Jerusalem to celebrate the
holy day. When they heard the commotion they came to
see what was going on. They were all surprised to hear
the apostles speaking their own languages.

"Aren't all these men from Galilee?" they asked. "Then how can they be telling the praises of God in our own language?" But some said, "They have just had too much wine."

128

Peter stood up in their defense. "These men are not drunk, this is what the prophet Joel wrote about: 'In the last days,' God says, 'I will pour out My spirit and they will prophesy.'"

129

"Listen to me, Jesus of Nazareth was a Man sent to you by God who worked wonderful miracles. But you had Him nailed to a cross. But God wasn't finished, He raised Jesus from the dead."

130

"We are witnesses that Jesus was raised from the dead and that God has put Jesus at His own right hand. Jesus has poured out the Holy Spirit, just as He promised. This is what you are seeing and hearing today."

131

"So, let all Israel be assured that God has made Jesus of Nazareth, the One you crucified, both Lord and Christ. He is the Messiah!"

132

All the people who heard Peter speak were deeply touched. They asked him and the other apostles, "What shall we do?"

Peter answered, "Each of you should repent and be baptized, in the name of Jesus Christ. Then your sins will be forgiven and you will receive the gift of the Holy Spirit."

134

There were many who accepted Peter's words that day and the apostles took them to a river and baptized them. About three thousand people were added to the group of believers that day.

The believers met together to listen to the apostles teach, and for fellowship with each other. They shared with any who had needs and spent time in prayer. Their hearts were filled with joy and praise for God.

A Lame Man Walks *Acts 3:1—4:3*

One afternoon Peter and John were on their way to the temple for a time of prayer.

They saw a man being carried to the temple gate called
"Beautiful". He sat there every day and begged from
those going into the temple.

138

Just as Peter and John were about to enter the temple, the man asked them for some money.

Peter looked at the man and said, "Look at us!" He did
so, expecting them to give him some money. Peter said, "I
don't have any money, but what I do have I will give you.
In the name of Jesus of Nazareth, get up and walk!"

140

Peter took the man's hand and helped him to his feet.
Miraculously the man's feet and legs were healed! He
jumped up and began walking around.

Then he went into the temple courts with Peter and John. He was walking and jumping and praising God. The people saw that this was the beggar who used to be crippled, and they were all amazed.

142

The people gathered around Peter, John, and the man. Peter said, "Why are you all surprised? It was not by our power or might that this man has been healed and can now walk."

"The God of Abraham, Isaac, and Jacob brought glory to His servant Jesus. But you gave Him over to be killed. You rejected the Holy and Righteous One, and instead asked for a murderer to be freed."

144

"But God raised Jesus from the dead. We are witnesses to this fact. This man was healed in the name of Jesus."

"Repent, then, and turn to God so that your sins may be wiped out and the Lord may give you times of refreshing, and that He may send the Christ, the one appointed for you; Jesus."

146

"The Lord God told Abraham, 'Through your descendants all people on earth will be blessed.' When God raised up His servant Jesus, He sent Him first to bless you by turning you away from your sins."

The priests and other religious leaders came up as Peter was speaking. They were angry to hear Peter talking about Jesus being raised from the dead, so they arrested Peter and John and put them in jail.

Stephen is Arrested *Acts 6*

The apostles were often beaten because they preached about Jesus and they were warned not to, but they kept on preaching. So the size of the group of believers grew and grew.

But then, some trouble came in their young church.
The Greek-speaking Christians thought their widows
were not being given as much food as the others in the
daily hand out of food.

150

So the apostles called a church meeting. They said, "Our job is to preach and we can't neglect that in order to hand out food. You choose seven men from the church to be in charge of handing out the food."

"Choose seven men who are well thought of, full of the Spirit and much wisdom. We will put them in charge of distributing the food. Then we apostles can spend our time in prayer and preaching God's Word."

152

The church agreed with this plan. They chose seven men: Stephen, Philip, Procorus, Nicanor, Timon, Parmenas, and Nicolas. They presented them to the apostles who laid their hands on them and prayed for them.

The apostles continued to preach God's Word and the number of disciples around Jerusalem increased. Even some of the Jewish priests became believers.

Stephen, who was one of the men chosen to pass out food, was a man full of God's grace and power. He even did many wonderful miracles among the people.

But, some men from the Synagogue of the Freedmen
started to argue with Stephen. However, none of them
could match Stephen's wisdom and faith.

156

So they found some men who would lie about Stephen.
They went around saying that they had heard him say
evil things about Moses and God.

The Jewish people and leaders believed the lies of these men. They grabbed Stephen and brought him before the Sanhedrin, which was like a court.

158

Some people stood before the Council and lied, "We have heard this man say that Jesus of Nazareth will destroy the temple and do away with all that Moses taught us."

Everyone was watching Stephen closely. What they saw
was a miracle! His face began to glow like the face of an
angel. Stephen was trusting God to take care of him.

Stephen is Stoned to Death Acts 7:1—8:1

Some Jews had told lies about Stephen in order to get him into trouble. Stephen was arrested and brought before the Sanhedrin. "Is it true that you said bad things about the temple and Moses?" they asked.

Stephen had a reply ready for them. "God appeared to our ancestor Abraham while he was still in Mesopotamia and said, 'Leave your country and go to a land I will show you.'"

162

"The land God sent him to is this land where you now live. But God did not give him any of this land. Instead God promised that Abraham's descendants would possess it, even though Abraham had no children yet."

"Abraham had a son named Isaac, who became the father of Jacob. Jacob had twelve sons, sometimes called the twelve patriarchs. These patriarchs sold their brother Joseph as a slave into Egypt."

164

"But God was with Joseph. He gave Joseph favor with those who ruled over him and such great wisdom that finally Joseph was made a ruler in Egypt. He eventually brought his father Jacob and his brothers to live in Egypt with him."

"Some years later, God was ready to keep His promise to Abraham. But then a pharaoh came into power who did not remember Joseph. This pharaoh was mean to the Israelites, so God sent Moses to free His people."

"God chose Moses to lead His people out of captivity. He also spoke to Moses up on the mountain and gave His commandments to Moses to pass on to the people. But our fathers would not obey Him."

"You heathens are just like your ancestors! You fight against the Holy Spirit. Your fathers killed the prophets, even the ones who spoke about the Righteous One—and you have killed that very Righteous One!"

168

The religious leaders in the Sanhedrin were very angry about these accusations from Stephen. But Stephen looked up toward heaven and said, "I see heaven open and the Son of Man standing at the right hand of God."

The people covered their ears and began to yell at the top of their lungs. They all rushed at Stephen and dragged him outside the city gates. Then they picked up big stones and threw them at Stephen.

170

Even while they were throwing the stones, Stephen prayed, "Lord Jesus, receive my spirit." He fell down to his knees shouting, "Lord, do not hold this sin against them."

This is the way Stephen died. The men who had stoned Stephen had given their coats to a man named Saul to hold, Saul did nothing to stop Stephen's death.

Philip Helps the Ethiopian *Acts 8:26-40*

Philip, one of the disciples, had been instructed by an angel to go to a certain road and wait there.

Philip waited by the road and after a while an Ethiopian man came along. This man was an important official in charge of the treasury of the queen of the Ethiopians.

174

The Ethiopian had been in Jerusalem to worship the Lord. Now, on his way home, he was sitting in his chariot reading from the book of Isaiah the prophet.

Philip was instructed by the angel to approach the Ethiopian. So Philip went up close to the chariot and he heard the man reading Isaiah out loud. Philip asked, "Do you understand what you are reading?"

176

"How can I," he answered, "without someone to explain it to me?" Then he asked Philip to ride along in the chariot.

The passage that the Ethiopian was reading was: "As a sheep led to the slaughter or a lamb before its shearer is dumb, so he opens not his mouth."

178

מֵעֹצֶר וּמִמִּשְׁפָּט לֻקָּח
וְאֶת־דּוֹרוֹ מִי יְשׂוֹחֵחַ
כִּי נִגְזַר מֵאֶרֶץ חַיִּים
מִפֶּשַׁע עַמִּי נֶגַע לָמוֹ ׃

"In his humiliation justice was denied him. Who can
describe his generation? For his life is taken up from
the earth."

"I don't understand who the prophet is talking about," the Ethiopian said. "Is he speaking about himself or someone else?"

180

Philip began with that passage of Scripture and using some others also, he told the Ethiopian the whole story of Jesus.

When he was finished the Ethiopian said, "Look, here is some water. Is there any reason why I cannot be baptized right now?"

182

He ordered the chariot to stop. Then Philip and the
Ethiopian went down into the water and Philip
baptized him.

When they came up out of the water, the Spirit of the Lord quickly took Philip away and the Ethiopian never saw him again. But the man went on his way praising God.

Saul's Conversion *Acts 9:1-19*

184

When Stephen had been stoned to death, the man who had kept the coats of the murderers was a man named Saul. Now Saul began to persecute the church in Jerusalem, throwing both men and women into jail.

Saul went to the high priest and asked for letters to the synagogues in Damasacus requesting their cooperation. He wanted to go there and arrest any Christians he found and bring them back to Jerusalem.

Saul got the letters he wanted and he started for
Damascus. But, just before he got to the city a brilliant
light from heaven flashed all around him.

Saul fell to the ground and he heard a voice say,
"Saul, Saul, why do you persecute Me?" "Who are
You, Lord?" Saul asked. "I am Jesus, whom you are
persecuting," the voice answered.

"Get up and go into the city," the Lord said. "You will be
told what you must do." The men who were with Saul
heard the sound, but didn't see anyone speaking. They
just stood there, speechless.

When Saul got up, he was blinded. His friends had to lead him into the city by the hand. He was blind for the next three days and he did not eat or drink anything.

190

Meanwhile the Lord spoke to one of His disciples in Damascus named Ananias. The Lord called to him in a vision, "Ananias!" "Yes, Lord," he answered.

The Lord said, "Go to the house of Judas on Straight Street and ask for a man named Saul. Saul is praying to Me right now and he has seen a vision of a man named Ananias laying hands on him so that he can see again."

192

Ananias was afraid. He said, "But Lord I have heard of the terrible things this man has done to the church in Jerusalem. Now he is in Damascus to round up the Christians here and arrest us."

The Lord told Ananias, "Go! This is the man I have chosen to carry My name to the Gentiles and all the people of Israel. I will show him how much he must suffer for My name."

194

So Ananias went to Saul and said, "Brother Saul, the Lord Jesus who appeared to you on the road, has sent me in order that you might be able to see again and be filled with the Holy Spirit."

Ananias laid his hands on Saul and immediately Saul's eyesight returned. He got up and was baptized, then after having some food his strength returned. This is how Saul, who was now called Paul, enemy of believers, became a servant of Jesus.

Peter Does Two Miracles *Acts 9:32-43*

When the persecution of the church began in Jerusalem, many of the apostles quietly remained in the city. But some of the disciples went to Judea and Samaria to share the good news about Jesus.

Peter traveled around the country preaching about Jesus. One time he went to visit the believers in the town of Lydda, a small town near Joppa.

While he was in Lydda Peter met a man named Aeneas.
This man was paralyzed. He had been in bed eight
years because he could not walk.

199

Peter said to him, "Aeneas, Jesus Christ heals you. Get up and make your bed!"

Aeneas got up immediately! All the people who lived in Lydda and Joppa saw him walking around and they became believers in Jesus Christ.

There was another disciple living in Joppa. Her name was Tabitha, which in Greek is Dorcas. This woman was always doing good things and helping the poor in whatever way she could.

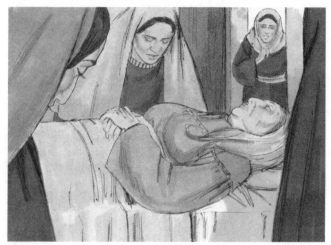

202

About the time that Peter was in Lydda, Dorcas became sick and died. Her friends sadly washed her body and placed it in an upstairs room.

When Dorcas' friends heard that Peter was in nearby Lydda, they sent two men to ask him to come to Joppa.

204

Peter arrived in Joppa and the believers took him to the room where Dorcas' body lay. The women there showed him the clothing that Dorcas had made for them and told him of her kindness.

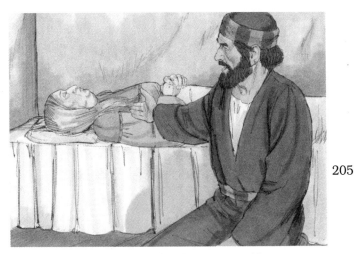

Peter asked everyone to leave the room and he got down on his knees and prayed. Then he turned to the dead woman and said, "Tabitha, get up."

206

She opened her eyes and when she saw Peter she sat up. Peter took her hand and helped her stand up.

Then Peter called the others in and presented Dorcas to them alive. The news of this miracle spread all over Joppa and many believed because of it. Peter stayed in Joppa with a man named Simon who was a tanner.

Peter Escapes from Prison *Acts 12:1-24*

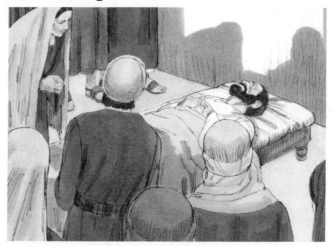

King Herod had arrested some believers in Jerusalem.
He had even put some of them to death; one of those
was the apostle James, the brother of John. He had
been killed with a sword.

King Herod saw that this pleased the people, so he went looking for more believers. He found Peter and had him arrested during the Feast of Unleavened Bread. The king planned to put him on trial after the Passover.

The members of the church in Jerusalem were worried about Peter and while he was in prison they prayed for him constantly. They met in the house of Mary, John Mark's mother.

The night before the trial, Peter was sleeping between two guards on the floor. Suddenly Peter was awakened by an angel of the Lord. "Quick, get up," the angel said and the chains fell off Peter's wrists.

212

"Follow me," the angel said. Peter followed him and they walked past the guards on duty, all the way out of the prison. They came to the iron gate of the prison and it opened by itself. Peter thought he was dreaming.

After the angel had walked out onto the street with
Peter, it disappeared. Then Peter realized that God had
sent the angel to rescue him.

214

Peter went right to Mary's house where the believers were gathered to pray for him. He knocked on the door.

It was answered by a servant girl named Rhoda. She recognized Peter's voice and got so excited that she ran to tell everyone that he was at the door, but she forgot to let him in.

216

The others in the house didn't believe Rhoda. They said,
"You're just dreaming," or "It must be Peter's angel."
But Rhoda kept insisting that it was Peter and Peter
kept on knocking on the door.

Finally someone else checked who was knocking and found out that it really was Peter. They were all amazed. Peter told them all to be quiet, then explained how the Lord had rescued him.

The next morning at the prison was chaos. They discovered that Peter was missing and they searched everywhere for him. When they could not find him, Herod had all the guards put to death.

Some time later Herod gave a speech to some people.
They shouted, "This is the voice of a god, not a man."
Herod accepted their praise and did not give it to God,
so an angel struck him down and he died.

Paul and Silas in Prison *Acts 16:13-40*

The apostle Paul had a vision in which he was told to go to Macedonia. So he was preaching in Philippi, the main city of that area. One woman, Lydia, and her entire household became Christians after hearing Paul preach.

One day Paul was on his way to a prayer meeting when he met a slave girl. She had an evil spirit in her which could tell the future.

The girl kept following Paul and his group around shouting, "These men are servants of God and they can tell you how to have your sins forgiven." She did this every day when she saw Paul.

Finally, Paul went to the girl and said, "Spirit, in the name of Jesus Christ, I command you to come out of this girl." At that very moment the evil spirit left the young girl.

The girl's owners were very angry because they had made a lot of money from her fortune telling. They grabbed Paul and Silas and dragged them to the marketplace where the judges were.

The judges heard the charges against them and had
them stripped, and beaten. Then they put them in prison
and told the jailer that if they escaped he would be killed.

The jailer took no chances and he put them in the
innermost cell and put their feet in stocks. Paul and
Silas prayed and sang hymns all night. The other
prisoners were listening to them.

Around midnight there was a great earthquake. The whole prison shook, the doors flew open and everyones chains fell off.

228

When the jailer woke up and saw all the doors open, he thought the prisoners were all gone. He was about to kill himself when Paul shouted, "Don't harm yourself. We are all here!"

229

The jailer was astonished. He brought Paul and Silas out and asked, "What must I do to be saved?" They replied, "Believe on the Lord Jesus Christ." They were able to share this with his entire family.

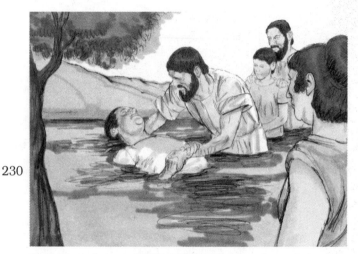

Even though it was still night, the jailer cleaned their wounds. Then they went to the river and the jailer and his whole family were baptized. They were full of joy because they believed in God.

The next day the judges said Paul and Silas could
go, but Paul wanted the judges to escort them out of
the city. On their way, they stopped at Lydia's house
to encourage her family in their faith, then they left
for Thessalonica.

Paul Speaks to the Areopagus *Acts 17:16-34*

Paul had been traveling around preaching in different cities. Now he was on his way to Athens, which was a city of great culture.

Paul walked around the city and noticed many statues and idols which the people worshiped. He spoke in the synagogues on Sabbath day to the Jews and to other people in the marketplace.

234

The Epicurean and Stoic philosophers listened to Paul and began to argue with him. Some said, "What is he babbling about?" Others said, "He seems to be talking about some foreign god."

235

So they asked Paul to come to a meeting of the
Areopagus, a great important council. "Now," they said,
"tell us what you are talking about. You are teaching
some things we have not heard before and we do not
understand."

Paul said, "Men of Athens, I can see that you are very religious. I have walked around your city and I saw many altars. I noticed one that had the inscription 'To an Unknown God.'"

237

"It is this God, whom you do not know, that I have been talking about. This is the God who made the world and all that is in it. Since He is the Lord of heaven and earth, He does not live in temples which men have built."

238

"He gives life and breath to all that lives. He has given us everything we have. He made all the people of the world from one man. Even one of your own poets wrote, "We are sons of God.""

"We are God's children and we should not think that He is like these idols. He is not made from silver or gold—He was not made by men."

240

"At one time, God ignored that kind of ignorance, but
no more. He wants us to repent and give up idols. We
should worship only Him."

"He has made a day for judging the world, by the Man He has chosen. He made this obvious by bringing that Man back to life."

Some of the philosophers laughed when Paul talked about a dead man coming back to life. But others said, "We want to hear more about this later."

After that Paul left the Areopagus. A few people came with him and believed. One was a man named Dionysius, a member of the Areopagus. Another was a woman named Damaris.

Paul's Final Instructions *1 - 2 Timothy, Titus*

Paul was captured and put in prison in Rome. He was held there for two years, then released. He continued to travel and preach about Jesus, often bringing friends along with him.

On one of his trips to Macedonia, he left his good friend Timothy in Ephesus and told him, "Stay here and try to stop those who are teaching wrong doctrines."

246

Another time he left Titus in Crete with these instructions, "Do what you can to strengthen the churches and appoint elders in every town who will follow instructions and lead good lives."

When Paul was in prison again, he wrote Timothy another letter. Paul was not discouraged. He wrote, "I am not ashamed, and I don't want you to be ashamed either, rather join with me in suffering for the gospel of God."

248

"I was appointed an apostle and teacher of this gospel, for that I am suffering. But I am not ashamed, I know that I can trust in the One I have believed in."

"My son, be strong in the grace that Christ Jesus gives you. Remember the things you have heard me teach, pass them on to other trustworthy men who can, in turn, teach them to others."

250

"You man of God, flee evil desires, pursue righteousness, faith, love and gentleness. Fight the good fight of
the faith. Keep yourself pure until the Lord returns."

"I urge you Timothy, preach the Word. Correct, discipline and encourage the people. Do this all with patience and careful instruction. You will have to suffer for your work, but do not leave anything undone."

"The time for my departure has come. I have fought a good fight, I have finished the race. I have kept the faith."

"Now the time has come for me to stop fighting and to rest. There is a crown of righteousness waiting for me in heaven which the Lord will give to me. That is not just for me, but to all who have waited for His return."

254

"At my first trial, I had no one to defend me, everyone left. But the Lord stood with me and gave me strength to preach so that the whole world might hear."

"The Lord saved me from being thrown to the lions. The Lord will continue to deliver me from evil, and will bring me safely into His heavenly kingdom. To God be the glory forever and ever. Amen."